THE GOSPEL
CONVERSATION

THE GOSPEL CONVERSATION

Engaging the Lost in Everyday Life

Sam Greer

ISBN: 1977904785
ISBN 13: 9781977904782

Contents

Foreword

People are talking. Conversations are taking place everywhere, all the time. People communicate one-on-one and also in groups. While the content of many conversations is shallow, conversations nevertheless are continuous.

The most important conversations are those that focus on the Gospel of Jesus Christ. Gospel conversations are the vehicles God uses to communicate His saving truths of: God's love for man, man's need for God, man's sinful state, Jesus' sacrificial atonement, repentance & faith, and the need to receive Christ by calling on His name in prayer. A believer in Jesus shares all of that with lost people when he communicates the Gospel.

In his new book, *The Gospel Conversation*, Pastor Sam Greer explains why Gospel conversations are significant, and also provides an easy-to-follow, step-by-step blueprint explaining how to have such conversations. He points out the fact that Jesus commanded *all* of His followers to share the Gospel and witness to lost people. If a Christian is not fishing for the souls of lost people, He is not following Jesus as closely as he should (cf. Matthew 4:19). *All* Christians should emulate Deacon Philip of the first century by opening our mouths and sharing what the Bible says about Jesus with lost people (cf. Acts 8:35). Dr. Roy Fish used to tell us at Southwestern Baptist Theological Seminary, "Men, you cannot serve Jesus with a zipped lip!" Likewise, Dr. Chuck Kelley, president of New Orleans Baptist Theological Seminary says, "If Jesus is in your heart, sooner or later He will come out of your mouth!"

Amen! Christians *must* verbally share the Gospel! What a joy it is to tell others about Jesus. May God use *The Gospel Conversation* to both inspire and instruct you in the delight and discipline of personal evangelism. Read and apply it, and God will help *you* to win precious souls to Jesus Christ.

Acts 1:8,

Steve Gaines, PhD
Senior Pastor, Bellevue Baptist Church, Memphis, TN
President of the Southern Baptist Convention

Introduction

On December 12, 2015, I finished the Rocket City Marathon in Huntsville, Alabama, at the age of forty-one. I barely missed the goal of running my first marathon by the age of forty. Training for a marathon consists of bitterly cold runs, humid and hot runs, early morning runs, mid-afternoon runs, evening runs, late night runs, short runs, and long runs. Remembering all the training runs is next to impossible; however, there is one training run I will never forget.

We visit my mother-in-law in Mississippi several times each year. The neighborhood where she resides offers a respectable two-mile run out to the main road. One hot, humid, summer morning, I took off on a four-mile run. Running in the summer humidity of south central Mississippi is like running in a sauna. As I was running—well, *running* may be a stretch. As I was jogging—well, *jogging* may be a leap. As I was rogging (a combination of running and jogging)—well, *rogging* may be an exaggeration. As I was walking—again, *walking* may even be up for debate. As I was moving, pouring sweat, panting for oxygen, and thirsting for something, anything, in liquid form, it happened.

Although I was moving slowly uphill for the final quarter mile of a four-mile run, anyone could tell that I was intentionally trying to exercise. Wearing ear buds was clear evidence that I was listening to jogging tunes. Wearing running shorts, a half-marathon t-shirt, and running shoes was clearer evidence that I was attempting to run. And the painful expression on my face was the clearest evidence that I was trying to jog. Being outside in the middle of a hot, humid day, it was plainly obvious that I was exercising.

Blanketed by the blazing sun and looking up from the bottom of the hill, I noticed a SUV coming over the crest. Immediately, the lady driving began to slow down. The next couple of minutes seemed to be right out of a movie, as if everything was moving in slow motion. The SUV pulled further over to my side of the road. It was so close I could feel the cool air sweep over my face as the driver's side backseat window rolled down. As the refreshing, crisp, cool air enveloped my blistering, red-hot face, an outstretched arm extended from the deep freezer-like coolness of the vehicle. In the hand of the outstretched arm was a mouth-watering 20-ounce soft drink. The thirst-quenching drink was covered with small drops of ice cascading down the sides and off the bottom of the bottle. The melting drops of ice almost sizzled as it touched down onto the scorching hot Mississippi pavement.

The sweet, middle-aged lady holding the soft drink, as if practiced a thousand times on a track relay team, handed me that cold, enticing, bottle in stride. I looked at her eyeball-to- eyeball and said, "Thank you." Being undeniably thirsty, I truly meant it. Before the grateful words left my lips, I heard the two ladies in the front seat say, "Wait, stop!" I stopped. The SUV stopped. The lady who handed me the soft drink asked, "Could you open this bottle for me?" What? *"Could you open this bottle for me?"* The only thing worse than running in the Mississippi humidity was holding that ice cold soft drink, only to open it and hand it back to its owner. As the SUV pulled away, I heard the ladies in the front seat laughing and saying, "He thought that drink was for him!"

What does it take to enter a gospel conversation? In John 4, Jesus was burdened for the lost Samaritan woman at the well. He was bold enough to share the living water, and He seized the opportunity by meeting the woman at the sixth hour. Jesus' actions at the well unveil three necessary elements of entering a gospel conversation: a burden for the lost, the boldness to declare the gospel, and the opportunity to share the gospel.

The trio of ladies in the SUV had a burden, had boldness, and seized an opportunity. Unfortunately for me, their burden was not for the thirsty, struggling jogger on the road. Rather, they were burdened for their own pleasure of consumption. The boldness they portrayed was legendary: Who stops a person from running and asks them to open a soft drink? What boldness! The ladies did not see me, nor did I see them until they topped the hill. The window of opportunity for such an encounter on that neighborhood road was small, and they took advantage. These ladies had what I needed, but they kept it to themselves.

As a follower of Jesus Christ, the conviction of the Holy Spirit reminds me that, in Christ, I have what a lost, thirsty, struggling, empty world needs. How often I have failed to offer the living water to men, women, boys, and girls whom I have encountered? May God have mercy on me! As a pastor, I was moved to write this book with the hope of equipping and encouraging Jesus' church to pursue gospel conversations.

In the book of Philemon, the apostle Paul starts a gospel conversation with his brother in Christ, Philemon, on behalf of his new brother in Christ, Onesimus. What can we learn from Paul's approach to entering this gospel conversation? The purpose of this book is to uncover the biblical basis of moving any and every conversation toward a gospel conversation. I invite you to take this journey with me as we biblically, intentionally, and practically enter gospel conversations. Remember, all gospel conversations start with a conversation. So, let's chat!

1

Gospel Transformation...

LEADS TO GOSPEL CONVERSATIONS

*"Therefore, O King Agrippa, I was not disobedient to the heavenly vision, but declared first to those in Damascus, then in Jerusalem and throughout all the region of Judea, and also to the Gentiles, that they should repent and turn to God, performing deeds in keeping with their repentance. For this reason the Jews seized me in the temple and tried to kill me. To this day **I have had the help that comes from God.**"* Acts 26:19-22

TRANSFORMED BY THE GOSPEL

B efore Paul wrote any letters as a follower of Christ, including Philemon, he collected letters from the high priest with the hopes of arresting followers of Christ in Damascus. On the road to Damascus, Saul the assassin was transformed into Paul the apostle by the gospel of Jesus. Before his transformation, Saul's testimony could be likened to, "I am helping Yahweh." After his transformation, Paul's testimony could be likened to, "Yahweh is helping me." Paul testified that since the day he was transformed by the gospel, he had the "help that comes from God."

Saul the assassin had quite a reputation as witnessed when Ananias, a disciple of Jesus, responded to Jesus' command regarding Saul. In Acts 9:11-13, the Bible says:

And the Lord said to him (Ananias), "Rise and go to the street called Straight, and at the house of Judas look for a man of Tarsus named Saul, for behold, he is praying, and he has seen in a vision a man named Ananias come in and

2

lay his hands on him so that he might regain his sight." But Ananias answered, **"Lord, I have heard from many about this man, how much evil he has done to your saints at Jerusalem."**

Saul the assassin was made different by the gospel so that Paul the apostle could make a difference for the gospel.

What is the gospel? The Greek word *evangelion*, transliterated as *the gospel,* means good news.[i] In 1 Corinthians 15:3, Paul described the gospel: "For I delivered to you as of first importance what I also received: that Christ died for our sins in accordance with the Scriptures, that he was buried, that he was raised on the third day in accordance with the Scriptures."

The gospel of Jesus is not good advice, good behavior, good deeds, good effort, good fortune, good genes, good habits, good intentions, good luck, good nature, good ole boys, good times, or good vibes. The gospel of Jesus is good news! David Platt defined the gospel this way:

The just and loving Creator of the universe has looked upon hopelessly sinful people and sent his Son, God in the flesh, to bear his wrath against sin on the cross and to show his power over sin in the Resurrection so that all who trust in him will be reconciled to God forever.[ii]

When a person arrives at the place of personal brokenness, there is no better time to consider the life, death, burial, resurrection, ascension, and return of Jesus. Have you arrived at the place of personal brokenness? Have you considered Jesus' cross? Have you considered His unrecognizable appearance, His uncontainable blood, His undeniable cross, His unavoidable death, His unprofitable enemy, His unbeatable Father, His unfathomable grace, His unstoppable hour, His unmistakable identity, His unthinkable judgment, His immeasurable love, His unimaginable paradise, His indisputable resurrection, and His unchangeable word? Have you been transformed by the gospel?

If you have not been transformed by the gospel, then stop right now and consider Jesus. Is the Holy

Spirit rebuking you of your sinful nature? If so, right now admit your sin and your desperate need for the Savior, for Jesus. Believe that God meant what He said and said what He meant about Jesus being raised from the dead. Confess Jesus as Lord of your life, and follow Him.

Tell somebody about your decision to repent and trust in Christ alone, by grace alone, through faith alone. Begin reading the Bible in the book of John. Start praying and don't stop. Make your decision public by baptism through immersion. Get connected with a Bible-believing, Bible-teaching, Bible-living local church. Connect in a small group and start sharing your life with other believers.

TRANSFERRING THE GOSPEL

In Acts 26:19-20, Paul the apostle told King Agrippa, "I was not *disobedient* to the heavenly vision, but *declared* first to those in Damascus, then in Jerusalem and throughout all the region of Judea, and also to the Gentiles, that they should repent and turn to God" (emphasis mine). Paul, after being transformed by the gospel, began declaring the gospel. For Paul, declaring the gospel was not a matter of convenience, but rather a matter of obedience. A transformed believer is being disobedient when failing to transfer the gospel.

Robby Gallaty, in his book *MARCS of a Disciple*, wrote, "Anybody whose life has been changed by professing faith in Christ possesses a built-in mechanism for sharing the Gospel."[iii] Ladies, if you know of a price-busting shoe sale, then you will tell your friends (please don't tell my wife Tonya). Men, if you catch a monster bass, then you will post a selfie from the boat. Social media has launched, to a higher level, a desire to be the first to share any news.

As followers of Christ, we should be just as passionate about sharing the good news of the gospel. When we are changed by the gospel, we should challenge others with the gospel. When we are delivered by the gospel, we should deliver the gospel. When we are found by the gospel, we should find others with the gospel. When we are given the gospel, we should give the gospel. When we are invited by the gospel, we should invite others to the gospel. When we are known by the gospel, we should make known the gospel. When we are remade by the gospel, we should relay the gospel. When we are spared by the gospel, we should share the gospel. When we are transformed by the gospel, we should transfer the gospel.

Believers should at least have a desire to declare the gospel. John Philips stated: "A person can be made to follow a given line of behavior from one of three reasons—out of a sense of discipline, out of a sense of duty, or out of a sense of desire. Discipline says, 'I have to'; duty says, 'I ought to'; desire says, 'I want to.'"[iv] Followers of Christ should share the gospel not out of discipline, duty, or merely desire, but out of devotion. Based on Phillips' description of discipline, duty, and desire, devotion may be thought of as, "I *get* to." How liberating for a devoted believer to be able to say, "I *get* to share the gospel!" May the power of the Holy Spirit move us from, "I *have* to," "I *ought* to," or even, "I *want* to share the gospel," and get us to the God glorifying place, "I *get* to share the

7

gospel." A follower of Christ gets to *share* the gospel with anyone, but gets to *save* no one.

TRANSITIONING TO THE GOSPEL

Once we are transformed by the gospel and devoted to sharing the gospel, how then, do we transition conversations to the gospel? Must every believer go to seminary to be equipped to transition to the gospel, attend a Bible college, or earn a degree in evangelism? The encounter between the Samaritan woman and Jesus offers some helpful application.

Jesus said to her, "Go, call your husband, and come here."

> The woman answered him, "I have no husband." Jesus said to her, "You are right in saying, 'I have no husband'; for you have had five husbands, and the one you now have is not your husband. What you have said is true." The woman said to him, "Sir, I perceive that you are a prophet. Our fathers worshiped on this mountain, but you say that in Jerusalem is the

place where people ought to worship." Jesus said to her, "Woman, believe me, the hour is coming when neither on this mountain nor in Jerusalem will you worship the Father. You worship what you do not know; we worship what we know, for salvation is from the Jews. But the hour is coming, and is now here, when the true worshipers will worship the Father in spirit and truth, for the Father is seeking such people to worship him. God is spirit, and those who worship him must worship in spirit and truth." The woman said, "I know that Messiah is coming (he who is called Christ). When he comes, he will tell us all things." Jesus said to her, "I who speak to you am he." So the woman left her water jar and went away into town and said to the people, **"Come, see a man who told me all that I ever did. Can this be the Christ?" Many Samaritans from that town believed in him because of the woman's testimony, "He told me all that I ever did."** John 4:16-26, 27-29, 39

After the Samaritan woman was transformed by the gospel, she did not enroll in seminary, go to a Bible college, earn a degree in evangelism, nor did she attend a Bible study. She went back into town and transitioned to the gospel by immediately sharing her own gospel transformation testimony. First, she began by sharing about a man who knew all about her, including her sin. Second, once she shared her testimony, she posed the question, "Can this be the Christ?" The Samaritan woman's gospel transformation testified to many, and many Samaritans believed. What a picture of transitioning to the gospel by starting with a gospel transformation testimony!

Phillips Brooks defined preaching as "the communication of *truth* through *personality*."[v] The same definition is helpful when applying the principle to personal witnessing. Truth has never changed, and never will. The truth of the gospel will never change. No two personalities are the same. Even personalities that have been transformed by the gospel are not the same. In this definition of preaching, that which remains the same, *truth*, and that which is never the same, *personality*, are connected by the word *through*. Every personality that has been transformed by the gospel and shares the truth of the gospel is powerful and effective.

Use the *personality* that God created and redeemed in you and share the *truth*. Don't be ashamed of your gospel transformation story. Don't fall into the trap that your gospel transformation story isn't colorful enough. Don't confuse colorful with powerful. The sin of man is what makes a testimony colorful, but the Son of God is what makes a testimony powerful.

The synoptic gospel writers Matthew, Mark, and Luke were created and redeemed with three distinct personalities, yet all three shared the same truth. Case in point, just before the death of Jesus on the cross, all three reported the darkness that fell over all the land. In Matthew 27:45, the Bible says, "Now from the sixth hour there was darkness over all the land until the ninth hour." In Mark 15:33, the Bible says, "And when the sixth hour had come, there was darkness over the whole land until the ninth hour." In Luke 23:44, the

Bible says, "It was now about the sixth hour, and there was darkness over the whole land until the ninth hour."

All three reported this miraculous phenomenon with one simple statement. Furthermore, none of them speculated, commentated, or guesstimated. If darkness fell over the whole earth from 12:00 noon to 3:00 p.m. today, then it would be a CNN Exclusive, a FOX News Alert, or MSNBC's Breaking News. Do these three titles even mean anything in today's world? No matter what time I turn on the news, it seems that all news is somehow breaking news, an exclusive, or an alert. The simple fact that these three distinct personalities refrained from embellishing the truth enhances the credibility of the truthfulness of the Word of God. Like the Samaritan woman and the synoptic gospel writers, followers of Jesus are set apart to be Jesus' witnesses by reporting the truth through personality.

Transition any and every conversation to a gospel conversation by sharing how God's story transformed your story. Talk about your life before Christ. Talk about how you came to Christ. Talk about your life since you came to Christ. In his book, *Share Jesus Like it Matters*, Steve Gaines penned, "Another tool for effectively sharing Jesus with a lost person is sharing your personal testimony of how Jesus saved you."[vi] Use your gospel transformation testimony to transition to the truth of the gospel. Robby Gallaty wrote, "Remember, in addition to the gospel message, believers wield a potent weapon: their personal testimony."[vii]

TRANSMISSION OF THE GOSPEL

In an article entitled, "The Crisis of Biblical Illiteracy and What We Can Do About It," Kenneth Berding wrote:

> Christians used to be known as "people of one book." Sure, they read, studied and shared other books. But the book they cared about more than all others combined was the Bible. They memorized it, meditated on it, talked about it and taught it to others. We don't do that anymore, and in a very real sense we're starving ourselves to death.[viii]

Gospel conversations take time to fully develop, especially in our biblically illiterate world. In such a time of biblical famine, building rapport in a relationship becomes even more important as one seeks to share the gospel. Entering a gospel conversation may take many conversations. So, what is the difference between a conversation and a gospel conversation? More specifically, what are the essential elements of a gospel conversation? Below are five essential elements of gospel conversations.

1. **Confess that Jesus is sinless.** Confessing that Jesus is sinless is essential to any gospel conversation. In John 1:1-2 & 14, the Bible says, "In the beginning was the Word, and the Word was with God, and the Word was God. He was in the beginning with God...And the Word became flesh and dwelt among us." As the second person of the Trinity, Jesus is God the Creator. A gospel conversation must start with the sinless Creator, who has revealed Himself in the person of the sinless Jesus.

In Hebrews 4:15, the author of Hebrews wrote, "For we do not have a high priest who is unable to sympathize with our weaknesses, but one (Jesus) who in every respect has been tempted as we are, yet without sin." As we confess Jesus as sinless, we must ask the Holy Spirit to convince an unbeliever that Jesus is right and he or she is wrong.

2. **Confess that your sins put Jesus to death.** Jesus, the sinless One, died a sinner's death. The apostle Paul wrote in Romans 6:23, "For the wages of sin is death, *but* the free gift of God is eternal life in Christ Jesus our Lord." Because of sin, we all deserve to die, BUT Jesus died for us, in our place, and instead of us.

We must confess that our sins are *sins*. The Bible never refers to our sins as mistakes, mishaps, or misunderstandings. Rather, the Bible refers to our commission and omission of sin as iniquity, transgression, sin, and evil. We must tell the person with whom we are sharing that we realize it was our sins that put Jesus to death.

3. **Confess your sins to Jesus.** After acknowledging that our sins put Jesus to death, we must share that we confessed our sins to God. As followers of Jesus, we must constantly confess our sins to God. In 1 John 1:9, the Bible says, "If we confess our sins, he is faithful and just to forgive us our sins and to cleanse us from all unrighteousness." Sharing the gospel must always involve declaring that we confess our sins to God.

4. **Confess that Jesus put your sins to death.** Although our sins put Jesus to death, Jesus' death put our sins to death. In 1 Peter 3:18, the Bible says, "For Christ also suffered once for sins...being put to death in the flesh...." Jesus stayed alive on this earth until the cross. Jesus stayed on the cross until His death. Jesus stayed in the tomb until His resurrection. The resurrected Jesus stayed on this earth until His ascension. Jesus will stay in heaven until His return. As we engage the lost in gospel conversations, we must confess that sins were put to death because Jesus stayed on the cross.

5. **Confess Jesus to sinners.** As we engage the lost in everyday life, we must confess Jesus to them. Jesus is the only hope for a lost, void, and thirsty soul. In fact, confessing Jesus is the way of salvation. Paul wrote in Romans 10:9, "If you confess with your mouth that Jesus is Lord and believe in your heart that God raised him from the dead, you will be saved." Let's join together and transmit the gospel by confessing Jesus to sinners.

TRANSPIRED BECAUSE OF THE GOSPEL

What transpires when we engage the lost in everyday life with the gospel? Some will believe and some will not believe. Some will want to hear more and some will not. Sometimes what transpires is the miraculous exponential sharing of the gospel in everyday life. Such was the case with David.

David was our Israeli tour guide on a ten-day Holy Land trip my wife Tonya and I took with Dr. Chuck Herring and his church. David is a Jew who was born and raised in Bronx, New York. After his parents died thirty-five years ago, he moved from New York to Israel, not knowing anyone. He has been a Holy Land tour guide for the past thirty-four years. David's historical, political, and cultural knowledge of Israel and the Jewish people is impressive. His witty and warm personality is inviting. By his own confession, David is not a follower of Jesus.

How do I know David is not a follower of Jesus? In her first conversation with David, Tonya asked him. In addition, David's historical and biblical explanations of the Holy Land sites proved his world view was not Christian.

One of the last tour stops was at the Garden of Gethsemane. David's explanation of what Jesus was going through in the Garden was unbiblical. He said that Jesus was having an identity crisis. He added that Jesus was trying to discover what His role was in His day. Was Jesus God? Was He man? Was He just a good teacher or a good prophet? David deduced that Jesus was trying to determine His identity as He wrestled with God.

As soon as David was finished speaking, Pastor Herring stepped forward and said: "Jesus was not having an identity crisis in the Garden of Gethsemane, rather He was having a redemption crisis."[ix] Jesus has never had an identity crisis. From the beginning of time, Jesus knew He was coming to the earth for the purpose of saving the lost. In the Garden of Gethsemane, Jesus was asking the Father that if there be another way for God's wrath to be satisfied and sinners to be justified, then let the cup of wrath pass from Him. Yet, Jesus always remained submissive to the Father's will.

After Pastor Herring shared the gospel truth, a miracle transpired. David approached Pastor Herring and myself, and this is the conversation that transpired:

David said, "Redemption crisis? I have never heard that before."

Pastor Herring responded, "David, Jesus is the only spiritual leader to make the audacious claim that He is the way and the truth and the life and no man comes to the Father but by Him. Buddha never made such a claim. Mohammed never made such a claim. Moses never made such a claim. Only Jesus made such a claim. When I think about all the dumb stuff I have done in my life, I am humbled to think that Jesus went to the cross and died for my sins. David, have you ever thought about your sin and who will pay the penalty for your sin?"[x]

Before dropping us off at the airport, David made this statement: "I would like to thank Dr. Herring for leading this trip. I have learned much from his teaching. In fact, I am going to begin teaching future groups that Jesus was having a redemption crisis not an identity crisis in Gethsemane."[xi] How did it transpire that an unbeliever will now be sharing the gospel as a tour guide? The exponential sharing of the gospel transpired because of a single gospel conversation.

The twenty-five verses of Philemon map out a biblical, intentional, and practical process of entering gospel conversations. Unpacking Philemon starts with the reality that gospel transformation leads to gospel conversations.

2

Gospel Conversations...

LEAD TO GOSPEL INVITATIONS

*Paul, a prisoner for Christ Jesus, and Timothy our brother. To Philemon our beloved fellow worker and Apphia our sister and Archippus our fellow soldier, and the church in your house: Grace to you and peace from God our Father and the Lord Jesus Christ. I thank my God always when I remember you in my prayers, because I hear of your love and of the faith that you have toward the Lord Jesus and for all the saints, and **I pray that the sharing of your faith may become effective for the full knowledge of every good thing that is in*** *us for the sake of Christ. For I have derived much joy and comfort from your love, my brother, because the hearts of the saints have been refreshed through you.*

Philemon 1-7

MAN-GIVEN RIGHT OR GOD-GIVEN RESPONSIBILITY

On July 7, 2016, Russian President Vladimir Putin signed a controversial anti-terrorism law that infringes on the rights of followers of Jesus to enter into gospel conversations. Regarding Russia's new law, the Barnabas Fund reported:

> The new law will require any sharing of the Christian faith—even a casual conversation— to have prior authorization from the state. This includes something as basic as an emailed invitation for a friend to attend church. Churches will also be held accountable for the activities of their members. So, if, for example, a church member mentions their faith in conversation

with a work colleague, not only the church member but also the church itself could be punished, with individuals facing fines of up to 50,000 rubles ($770).[xii]

A gospel conversation will never begin without a casual conversation. In Russia, entering a gospel conversation is no longer a right. In America, entering a gospel conversation remains a man-given right. More than a man-given right, for believers, entering a gospel conversation is a God-given responsibility. American believers must take advantage of the current man-given right to enter a gospel conversation in order to fulfill their God-given responsibility. So, what is the first step to entering a gospel conversation? Talk to people.

TALK TO PEOPLE

Has text messaging and social media damaged the art of conversation? Janet Sternberg, Professor of Communication and Media Studies at Fordham University in New York, said, "It (conversation) is an art that's becoming as valuable as good writing."[xiii]

If social media has not outright damaged the art of conversation, then it has increased its value. Using the emerging technology of his day, letter writing, Paul communicated the gospel of Jesus conversationally. He incorporated two important elements of the art of conversation: content and tone.

First, *what* Paul said was important. Paul's content mattered. He introduced himself as "Paul, a *prisoner* for Christ Jesus" (emphasis mine). Paul was in a Roman prison, but he was not a mere Roman prisoner. He was a prisoner of Jesus Christ who happened to be in a Roman prison. He had been arrested by the gospel of Jesus.

Paul wrote four more letters while in prison whereby he referred to himself as a *servant* or an *apostle*: Ephesians, Colossians, Philippians, and 2 Timothy. Only in Philemon does he present himself as a *prisoner*. Why? Gospel reconciliation was the heartbeat of Paul's penning the book of Philemon. He knew the importance of identifying with both Philemon and Onesimus for the sake of reconciliation. Paul is identifying with Onesimus as a slave while appealing to Philemon's compassion rather than his compulsion.

True reconciliation can only happen through reconciliation to the gospel, by the gospel, and through the gospel. Paul, then, identified and sympathized with both men. The content of *what* Paul is saying is for the sake of the gospel. Paul was able to speak to these men because he was willing to listen. Paul knew *what* to say because he knew *how* to listen. Paul could use his tongue effectively because he used his ears effectively.

When considering *what* Paul said, what can be learned about entering into a gospel conversation? Making a decision to talk to people means one must first listen to people. Speaking into a person's situation means one must first listen to a person's situation. In short, seek to speak to a person, not at a person.

Second, *how* Paul said what he said was important. Paul's tone mattered. "Grace to you and peace" captured the tone of *how* Paul communicated the gospel. Under this gracious greeting, Paul entered a gospel conversation in the context of an estranged relationship.

What can be learned from *how* Paul said what he said? A person's tone can make all the difference in a conversation. Gospel conversations are no exception. Standing on a street corner and yelling "Turn or burn" at people through a megaphone is terribly ineffective. Speaking the truth in a gracious way is powerfully effective.

Social media makes available more opportunities to enter gospel conversations. The challenge, however, is found in the fact that tone can be difficult to discern. Even with emoticons, it can be difficult to determine when a person is joking or serious, sarcastic or angry. Like Paul, believers should take advantage of every opportunity to enter a gospel conversation. At the same time, some conversations need to be conducted face to face. In 2 John 12, John wrote: "Though I have much to write to you, I would rather not use paper and ink. Instead, I hope to come to you and talk face to face." Talk to people face to face.

Be intentional about eating, shopping, and playing at the same locations for the purpose of building relationships with employees and fellow patrons. Ask for people's names. Call them by name as you ask about their families. Ask how you can pray for them, and then do it. After you pray, follow up with them by asking about the situation for which you prayed. Set up a time with them when you can share your story. Talk to people.

TALK TO GOD ABOUT PEOPLE

In Philemon 4, Paul stated, "I thank *my* God always when *I* remember you in *my* prayers" (emphasis mine). Responsible Bible students will pay attention to pronouns. The personal pronouns, *my* and *I*, suggest that Paul was in a relationship with God. He talked to God. He talked to God about people. He talked to God about the people to whom he was talking.

As a pastor, God has blessed me with the opportunity to serve three separate churches. In all three churches, one of the ways I got myself into most trouble involved the prayer list. By adding a name too late or removing a name too early, I inadvertently added my name to the church's naughty list. People can become very angry about who is or is not on the prayer list. Paul's prayer list was his prayer life. He didn't suddenly add Philemon or Onesimus to his prayer list. He to God about both men as he thought of them.

Paul didn't tell Philemon and Onesimus he would pray for them; he prayed for them. Don't say you will pray, just pray! Take the time you spend telling a person you will pray for them and instead pray for them in that moment. Talk to God about the people to whom you are talking.

Philemon and Onesimus knew that Paul prayed for them. How did they know? Paul told them. It is important to pray for people, and it is just as important to tell people you are praying for them. Rather than having to tell someone that *you are going to pray for them*, how much more effective to be able to say *I am praying for you*. Paul told the people for whom he prayed that he was already praying for them.

Paul prayed for people, he told people he prayed for them, and he told people *what* he prayed for them. In Philemon 6, Paul revealed, "I pray that the sharing of your faith may become effective for the full knowledge of every good thing that is in us for the sake of Christ." Telling people *what* you are praying gives opportunity to go deeper in conversation.

Every Sunday morning, I receive a text message from a particular lay leader in the church where I serve as pastor. Like clockwork, this brother in Christ shares he is praying for me. I know he really is praying because each Sunday, he texts *what* he prays. Each text is a different prayer, and I look forward to his message every week.

An accountability partner is key to talking to God about people. Identify a person or persons in your sphere of influence whom you need to engage in a gospel conversation. Find an accountability partner who is willing to do the same in his or her sphere of influence. Share those names with your accountability partner and join in prayer for each person. Pray for the people in each sphere of influence by name. Ask God to give you and your accountability partner the opportunity to share the gospel with each person. Follow up with one another, encourage one another, and hold one another accountable.

Let's recap what it looks like to talk to God about people. Don't say you *will* pray. Pray! Start praying for people in the moment and stop telling them you *will* pray. When you pray, tell them *what* you pray! Gospel conversations result from conversations with God. Talk to God about people.

TALK TO PEOPLE ABOUT THE GOSPEL

In Philemon 6, Paul says, "I pray that the sharing of your faith may become effective for the full knowledge of every good thing that is in us for the sake of Christ." What do you think he means with these words? *Every good thing* would include repentance, regeneration, salvation, justification, sanctification, glorification, faith, forgiveness, love, joy, peace, patience, kindness, goodness, faithfulness, gentleness, and self-control. *Sharing of your faith* would include fellowship, discipleship, worship, missions, service, and personal evangelism.

Paul argued that the *sharing of your faith* leads to *every good thing that is in us for the sake of Christ.* Personal evangelism, life-on-life evangelism, and relational evangelism all should incorporate the use of gospel conversations. As Stephen Lutz wrote, "Friendship evangelism that never gets to the gospel is neither friendship nor evangelism."[xiv]

A practical gospel tool is helpful when engaging the lost in everyday life, relationships and friendships. Many effective gospel tools are available. I was trained to share the gospel using the Roman Road, Evangelism Explosion, the Four Spiritual Laws, and FAITH. Each of these are effective and helpful.

As a pastor, I developed a holistic tool, known as CAST, to train churched people to share the gospel. The purpose of CAST is to help believers share their personal testimony through God's story. CAST is designed to share one story, through one verse of Scripture with one person. Each letter in CAST stands for a timeless truth essential to the gospel.

The Creator brought life with no end. The **"C"** stands for **Creator.** People need to know that there is a Creator who created everything. People need to know that God made them and God loves them. People need to know that they were created in the image of God. In the beginning, God brought life with no end.

The Act brought death with no end. The **"A"** stands for **Act.** God told Adam not to eat the fruit from the tree of the knowledge of good and evil or he would die. Adam and Eve ate from the tree which God had forbidden. Adam and Eve died. People need to know that they are sinners by nature and by choice.

The Sacrifice brought death to an end. The **"S"** stands for **Sacrifice.** Even while passing out the punishment for the act of disobedience, God promised the cure for the curse of death. The only verse that is required to use CAST to share the gospel is John 3:16, which says, "For God so loved the world, that he gave his only Son, that whoever believes in him should not perish but have eternal life." After sharing about the sacrifice, a person who is using the CAST tool would insert his or her testimony of trusting in Jesus.

The Turn brings life with no end. The **"T"** stands for **Turn.** After sharing John 3:16 and inserting one's personal testimony, the believer is now ready to ask for a response. The turn is all about repentance or making a 180-degree turn in one's life. God desires people to repent, commands people to repent, allows people to repent, and even saves people who repent. CAST is about sharing one's story using one verse with one person for the glory of God. The CAST process may take many conversations to get to the point of asking for a response.

God expected Philemon to talk to people about the gospel. God expects us to talk to people about the gospel. Paul did not ask, beg, command, demand, or pray for Philemon to share his faith. Paul prayed for the sharing of Philemon's faith be effective. He believed that believers in Christ talk to people about Christ. A follower of Christ who does not share the gospel is an oxymoron.

The gospel of Jesus Christ is what moves people in the church to be the Church. If you need to be reconciled with another brother or sister in Christ, then talk to them about the gospel. If a person needs to be reconciled to God, then talk to them about the gospel. You'll never connect the wrong person to Jesus!

BE A GOSPEL CONVERSATIONALIST

Do you enjoy engaging in and contributing to conversations? If so, you should consider yourself a conversationalist. If not, you can still be a gospel conversationalist. How? A gospel conversationalist is as much a good listener as a contributor to and engager in conversations. When you listen well, you can share well. As you listen to the other person, pray that God will give you an inroad to the gospel. The work of a gospel conversationalist involves being biblical, intentional, conversational, respectful, understandable and practical. Being a gospel conversationalist is work, but it works.

Be biblical. When you have the opportunity to share your testimony in a conversation, guard against putting more emphasis on your words than on God's Word. Your words can change no one, but God's Word can change anyone. As you share about mankind's fallen condition before a Holy God, insert Scripture about sin. As you share about God's love, sacrifice, and grace, insert Scripture about salvation. As you share about confession and repentance, insert Scripture about obedience.

Be intentional. Prior to surrendering to vocational ministry, I worked as an insurance agent. I was selling health insurance, life and disability insurance, long-term care insurance, and individual retirement accounts. Being a self-employed, commission-only agent taught me to build a strong pipeline of business contacts. Some people in my business pipeline were already clients, some were in the process of becoming clients, and others were prospective clients. Keeping the business pipeline full with people at each of these three stages was always the goal.

Do you have a gospel conversation pipeline? Do you have people with whom you've already shared the gospel, others with whom you are in the process of sharing the gospel, while others are prospects with whom you hope to share the gospel? Build your gospel conversation pipeline!

Be conversational. At the age of twenty-one, the Holy Spirit called out my sin through the power of God's Word. I believed the gospel and received the gift of forgiveness through Jesus Christ. A local associate pastor led me to Christ through an evangelistic tool known as the Roman Road. God gave me a desire to share my newfound faith in Christ.

The very first time I witnessed to someone was a disaster. In 1995, walked into a local VHS video rental store on Front Street in small town Crystal Springs, Mississippi. One of my friends from school worked in this store where people actually walked up and down aisles, looking for a movie to rent. The timing of my attempt to share Jesus was terrible, as it was on a Friday night. The store was packed. My friend was busy. I approached my friend, as nervous as I have ever been, and said something like, "I just trusted in Jesus as my Savior. I want to tell you that we are all sinners. We all deserve to die because of our sin. But the gift of God is eternal life through Jesus Christ. If you will confess with your mouth that Jesus is Lord, and believe in your heart that God raised Him from the dead, you will be saved." I turned around and walked out.

What a disaster! I didn't say hello. I didn't ask how it was going. I didn't allow my friend to even speak. The first time I shared the gospel was not conversational, but confrontational. I sounded preachy and judgmental, not genuine or humble. My friend wasn't able to engage and could not take me seriously. Because of my poor timing, I did a disservice not only to him, but to the testimony of Jesus Christ. Being conversational in one's approach to share Jesus will allow for more people to be reached.

Be respectful. Followers of Jesus are never able to force others into a relationship with Jesus. Pushing people into heaven is impossible, but pushing people away from heaven happens all the time. People begin a relationship with Jesus and will one day enter heaven only through belief and repentance. Remember, the gospel conversation you have with a person doesn't need to be their last. Leave the conversation in such a way that the person will be open for the next gospel conversation the Holy Spirit brings their way.

Be understandable. Avoid using churched language like *get saved, born again, invite Jesus into your heart, or propitiation of our sins* without explaining these phrases. Use biblical language in a way that is understandable.

Be practical. How many people in the local church go out for lunch after corporate worship on Sunday? How many potential gospel conversations are left on the table every Sunday? I challenge the church at Red Bank Baptist to start a gospel conversation with their waiter at lunch after church. Waiters are busy and are not standing around waiting to have a gospel conversation. Yet, any follower of Christ can be intentional and take advantage of the short time at lunch to start a gospel conversation. How? Take advantage of the natural times when your waiter will come to your table.

First, introduce yourself. Most of the time, when you are seated in a restaurant, your waiter will introduce him or herself and take your drink order. Take the opportunity to address your waiter by name and immediately introduce yourself as well. Don't wait until they return with the drinks. The reactions you receive from your waiter when you introduce yourself may be surprising. Recently, when our party introduced ourselves to our waiter, she responded: **"Wow! No one has ever introduced themselves to me before."**

Second, ask how you can pray for him or her. When your waiter returns with your drinks, he or she will probably ask to take your order. After all the orders are taken and before your waiter goes to place your order, call him or her by name and say, ***"We are about to pray over our food, and we want to know in what way we can pray for you."*** Be sure to ask ***in what way*** you can pray. Don't simply ask, "Can we pray for you," but, "**How** can we pray for you?" Don't wait until your food comes to ask **how** you can pray because your waiter may not be the server who delivers your food to the table.

Third, thank your waiter for reminding you how to serve Jesus and others. Here is the point by which you are starting a gospel conversation. So far, you have talked to your waiter, talked to God about your waiter, and now you are about to start a conversation about the gospel with your waiter. Tell your waiter that you are a follower of Jesus and thank him or her for serving in a way that reminds you to serve and not be served. Waiters do very little standing around and waiting; they are taking drink orders, bringing bread or appetizers to tables, filling empty drinks, delivering food, taking orders, and settling tabs. So making the connection with Jesus' followers being servants will be easy for them to understand. What a reminder for followers of Jesus! As we eagerly await the second appearing of Jesus, we should be serving Jesus and others.

Fourth, tip well! Please don't talk to your waiter, talk to God about your waiter, start a gospel conversation with your waiter, and leave a terrible tip. Here is a tip: tip well!

Fifth, revisit for further conversations. Make a note of the day and time you're eating so you can return and request the same waiter. Remember his or her name. Upon returning, ask your waiter about the issue you prayed over on your prior visit. Continue to build a relationship so that eventually you can set up a time when he or she is not working to share your story through the gospel.

Responses from your waiters may surprise you, but your intentionality to connect will surprise them. Some of the responses I have heard from waiters include: **"I have been looking for a church home. What church do you attend?" "Thank you for praying for me." "I am a single mom, and I am struggling to provide for my children. Please pray for me." "I am a college student, and I need direction on what field to study. Please pray**

for direction." "I am a Christian, but I feel far from God. Please pray for me."

Remember, being a gospel conversationalist is work, but it works. Gospel conversations start with a conversation. Talk to people. Gospel conversations result from conversations with God. Talk to God about the people with whom you are talking. Gospel conversations materialize as we converse with people about God. Talk to people about the gospel. The next section of Philemon reveals that gospel conversations lead to gospel invitations.

3

Gospel Invitations...

"Accordingly, though I am bold enough in Christ to command you to do what is required, yet for love's sake **I prefer to appeal to you—I, Paul, an old man and now a prisoner also for Christ Jesus—I appeal to you for my child, Onesimus,** *whose father I became in my imprisonment. (Formerly he was useless to you, but now he is indeed useful to you and to me.) I am sending him back to you, sending my very heart. I would have been glad to keep him with me, in order that he might serve me on your behalf during my imprisonment for the gospel,*

*but I preferred to do nothing without your consent in order that your goodness might not be by compulsion but of your own accord. **For this perhaps is why he was parted from you for a while, that you might have him back forever, no longer as a slave but more than a slave, as a beloved brother**—especially to me, but how much more to you, both in the flesh and in the Lord."*

Philemon 8-16

UNENGAGED NATIONS TO
UNCHURCHED NEIGHBORS

I will never forget his words. Pastor George Tanya Mbongko of Pillar and Buttress Ministry in Cameroon, Africa said, "One Bangante Cameroonian coming to Christ is equivalent to one-hundred Muslims coming to Christ."[xv] The Bangante people of Cameroon are deceived by the darkness of ancestral worship known as the worship of the skulls.

Skull worship consists of family members burying their dead only to dig them up a year later. Upon exhuming the dead, the family removes the skulls and places them in clay pots or house-like tombs in their homes. Removing the skulls of ancestors, placing them in the home, and feeding them is based upon the belief that appeasing the ancestors of the skulls will keep evil away. The Bangante believe that improper care of ancestral skulls leads to ancestral wrath, family illness, infertility, or even death.[xvi]

In preparation to preach at the January 2016 Peace Rally in Bangante Cameroon, I listened to the pastors in Bangante share about the darkness of skull worship. Prior to the first night of the rally, I was overcome as the pastors shared that nearly every home in Bangante was full of skulls. While sitting on the preaching platform worshiping with those pastors, God moved my heart to the rich man and Lazarus text in Luke 16:19-31. God gave me a specific word to preach to the hundreds of Bangante people gathered that night.

When the rich man and Lazarus died, immediately, they were both alive. One was alive in Hades. One was alive at Abraham's side. In Luke 16:22-25, the Bible says:

The poor man died and was carried by the angels to Abraham's side. The rich man also died and was buried, and in Hades, being in torment, he lifted up his eyes and saw Abraham far off and Lazarus at his side. And he called out, '**Father** Abraham, have mercy on me, and send Lazarus to dip the end of his finger in water and cool my tongue, for I am in anguish in this flame.' But Abraham said, **'Child**, remember that you in your lifetime received your good things, and Lazarus in like manner bad things; but now he is comforted here, and you are in anguish. And besides all this, between us and you a great chasm has been fixed, in order that those who would pass from here to you may not be able, and none may cross from there to us.'

The rich man's use of "father" and Abraham's use of "child" offered a Holy Spirit-inspired opportunity for practical gospel application. Often, I have pondered the use of these two familial terms in the context of Luke 16. As I was sitting on the Peace Rally platform, while praying over the Bangante people enslaved by ancestral worship, God gave me this clear insight.

The reason the rich man referred to Abraham as father was because Abraham was his Jewish ancestor. The reason Abraham referred to the rich man as child was because the rich man was his Jewish descendant. To hear the ancestor of ancestors, Abraham, tell his descendant, "between us and you a great chasm has been fixed" is a terrifying truth. Basically, the rich man was being told that his ancestor could do nothing for him.

Standing before the Bangante people I said:

If the ancestor of ancestors, Abraham, was unable to do anything for his descendant, then your ancestors are unable to do anything for you. But there is One who said, 'Before Abraham was I AM.' Jesus wants you to know that before the ancestor of ancestors was, He said, 'I AM.' Jesus wants you to know that He put skull worship to death through His death at the place called the Skull. Jesus invites you to forsake skull worship and trust in Him alone as your Savior and follow Him as Lord.

Some accepted the invitation, some did not.

The opportunity to extend a practical gospel invitation to the Bangante people was the result of having a gospel conversation with those Bangante pastors. Gospel conversations lead to gospel invitations. Gospel chats lead to gospel invitations. Gospel dialogues lead to gospel invitations. Gospel talks lead to gospel invitations.

Undoubtedly, gospel conversations lead to gospel invitations in unengaged nations. Do gospel conversations lead to gospel invitations among our unchurched neighbors here in the United States? Sadly, only 2% of the churched invite the unchurched to church, while 80% of the unchurched would come to church if invited by the churched.[xvii] Unengaged does not mean unengageable. Unchurched does not mean unchurchable. Unreached does not mean unreachable. So, let's be unashamed and invite the unchurched, unengaged, and unreached! Gospel invitations will never happen absent gospel conversations.

THE GOSPEL INVITES

In Philemon 9-10, Paul wrote, "...*for love's sake I prefer to appeal to you*—I, Paul and old man and now a prisoner also for Christ Jesus—*I appeal* to you for my child, Onesimus" (emphasis mine). For the sake of the gospel, Paul appealed to Philemon on behalf of Onesimus. The Greek word transliterated as "I appeal" also means "I invite."[xviii] Paul communicated that the very nature of the gospel is to invite. In John 3:17, the Bible says, "For God did not send his Son into the world to condemn the world, but in order that the world might be saved through him." The gospel does not condemn, the gospel invites.

Paul mentioned his imprisonment four different times in Philemon. Perhaps he referenced his imprisonment multiple times to remind Philemon of a gospel opportunity with Onesimus. Philemon was unable to free Paul from his Roman chains; however, Philemon was able to free Onesimus from his slave chains. The gospel invites people to be set free. The gospel invited Paul to be set free. The gospel invited Philemon and Onesimus to be set free. In Romans 8:15, Paul wrote, "For you did not receive the spirit of slavery to fall back into fear, but you have received the spirit of adoption as sons, by whom we cry, 'Abba! Father!'" The gospel invites those enslaved by sin to become children of God.

God sent someone to set you free with the gospel, and in turn, God wants to send you to set someone free with the gospel. Who do you need to set free from the chains of bitterness and unforgiveness? Who do you need to set free with gospel benevolence, gospel conversations, gospel deliverance, gospel encouragement, gospel forgiveness, gospel giving, gospel hope, gospel invitations, gospel joy, gospel kindness, gospel love, gospel missions, gospel news, gospel obedience, gospel prayers, gospel proclamation, gospel reconciliation, gospel service, or gospel truth? The gospel invites.

THE GOSPEL INVITES THE UNINVITED

Paul's gospel conversation with Onesimus led to a gospel invitation. In Philemon 10, Paul identified Onesimus as "my child" and referred to himself as Onesimus' father. Apparently, Paul led Onesimus to Christ. As a runaway slave, Onesimus would qualify as the uninvited. Philemon's blood must have boiled as he read Paul's words. As Onesimus' owner, Philemon had every right to punish or even execute Onesimus for running away.

Onesimus' situation was only half of the equation that qualified him to be uninvited. Regarding the relationship between Philemon and Onesimus, Paul acknowledged "formerly he was *useless* to you" (Philemon 11) (emphasis mine). Onesimus' name means "useful."[xix] Yet, formerly, he was useless. What qualified Onesimus to be uninvited? Onesimus was not a son; he was a slave. Worse than a slave, he was a runaway slave. Worse than a runaway slave, he shamed his own name by opposing its meaning. In light of his running away, Philemon must have been surprised to hear from Onesimus again.

When my phone rang one Wednesday afternoon, I was surprised to hear the voice on the other end. To earn my PhD in Preaching from New Orleans Baptist Theological Seminary, I was required to write a dissertation on some aspect of preaching, and I chose the preaching of David Jeremiah, specifically sermon application. As a part of the research, I wanted to interview Dr. Jeremiah over the phone. I called his assistant and left a message. Months passed, and I received no return call. Meanwhile, other dissertation students shared how helpful it was to interview their respective preachers.

Eleven months after leaving a message, my phone rang. By this time, I had given up hope of hearing from Dr. Jeremiah, and I did not recognize the number. I answered, saying, "This is Sam." The voice on the other end said, "Hey Sam, this is David Jeremiah." Immediately, I responded, "Yeah, right. Hey David." My initial thought was one of the other students was pretending to be Dr. Jeremiah. As the conversation continued, I embarrassingly realized this really was David Jeremiah. I was surprised to hear from him!

Certainly, Philemon was surprised to hear from Onesimus. According to Paul's acknowledgment, it was no secret that Onesimus was useless to Philemon. When Philemon read that Onesimus was now useful, fulfilling the meaning of his name, he may have been shocked.

Like the lame, sinners, tax collectors, blind, crippled, and lepers, Onesimus qualified as the uninvited. Have you ever been part of the uninvited? Do you know someone who may be viewed as the uninvited? Who is the Onesimus in your life? The gospel of Jesus invites the lame, the least, and the lost. The gospel of Jesus invites those who are locked up and those who are looking. The gospel of Jesus invites the Onesimus in your life. The gospel invites the uninvited.

THE GOSPEL INVITES THE INVITED TO BE INVITERS

Paul's gospel conversation with Philemon led him to invite Philemon to extend a gospel invitation of reconciliation to Onesimus. In Philemon 15-16, Paul appealed to Philemon on behalf of Onesimus: "For this perhaps is why he was parted from you for a while, that you might have him back forever, *no longer as a bondservant but more than a bondservant, as a beloved brother*" (emphasis mine). Both Onesimus and Philemon were set free by the gospel. No longer are they merely in a contentious slave and master relationship. Now they are beloved brothers in Christ. Paul invited Philemon, the invited, to be an inviter, and invite the uninvited, Onesimus.

The relationship, or lack thereof, of the two brothers in the parable of the prodigal son provides an insightful parallel to the relationship between Onesimus and Philemon. In Luke 15:30-32, the Bible says, "'But when *this son of yours* came, who has devoured your property with prostitutes, you killed the fattened calf for him!' And he said to him, 'Son, you are always with me, and all that is mine is yours. It was fitting to celebrate and be glad, for *this your brother* was dead, and is alive; he was lost, and is found'" (emphasis mine).

Speaking to his father, the older brother referred to the younger, rebellious son not as his brother, but as "this son of yours." When the prodigal son returned home, the fattened calf was killed and he immediately went from being a hired servant to a beloved son. The father referred to the younger, rebellious son not as "this son of mine," but rather, "this your brother." Upon encountering Onesimus, Paul shared the Lamb of God, who takes away the sin of the world, not a fattened calf. Onesimus believed God. He repented of his sin. He confessed Jesus as Lord. He became more than a slave. He became a child of God and a beloved brother to Philemon.

Just as the father in the parable of the prodigal son invited the older son to extend an invitation of reconciliation to his younger brother, Paul is inviting Philemon to extend an invitation to Onesimus. How can we know that Paul is extending such an invitation to Philemon? In other words, how can we know that the gospel is inviting the invited to become an inviter? In nine verses, from Philemon 8 to Philemon 16, the second-person singular, personal pronoun "you" is used thirteen times. The Holy Spirit makes clear that is the responsibility of Philemon, as well as all who proclaim Christ as Savior, to be inviters by inviting the uninvited.

Even the uninvited, when invited, are invited to be inviters. Like Onesimus, the Samaritan woman qualified as the uninvited. In a first century Jewish culture, she was viewed as the uninvited because she was a woman, a Samaritan, and an outcast in her own community. Jesus intentionally invited her to Himself. As a result, the Samaritan woman was invited to be an inviter. In John 4:29, the Samaritan woman returned to town and said, "Come, see a man who told me all that I ever did. Can this be the Christ?"

Gospel conversations lead to gospel invitations because the gospel invites, the gospel invites the uninvited, and the gospel invites the invited to be inviters. The next text, Philemon 17-20, uncovers that gospel invitations lead to gospel celebrations.

4

Gospel Celebrations...

So if you consider me your **partner, receive him as you would receive me**. If he has wronged you at all, or owes you anything, **charge that to my account. I, Paul, write this with my own hand: I will repay it**—to say nothing of your owing me even your own self. Yes, **brother, I want some benefit from you in the Lord. Refresh my heart in Christ.**

Philemon 17-20

TAKING PERSONAL EVANGELISM PERSONALLY

Paul became all things to Philemon and won him to Christ. Paul became all things to Onesimus and won him to Christ. Let's become all things to all people that we might win people to Christ, as well. Let's be approachable, benevolent, caring, forgiving, giving, hospitable, kind, loving, patient, and truthful. If we are going to personally win anyone to Christ, we must take personal evangelism personally. God moved me to take entering a gospel conversation with my neighbor Suman personally.

Suman and his Hindu family are from India, and live five doors down from my family. The Holy Spirit burdened my heart for Suman, his family, and Hindus in India. I am praying that God will allow me to become all things to Suman that he might be won to Christ. Through conversations with Suman, I realized that the door to Suman's home, just five doors from my own, may be the gateway for the gospel to reach India.

Suman and I have spoken on many occasions. He has shared much about his family back in India. We have discussed family, marriage, work, hobbies, religion, and holidays. Most recently, we conversed about his desire to move his family back to India. What an opportunity! May God grant the opportunity for Suman to receive the gospel so he can take the gospel back to India. Speaking of his desire to move back to his country, he said that in three years, he's planning to move his family back to India. He's waiting until then because in three years, he will receive U.S. citizenship and be able to travel more freely as a dual citizen.

Sharing the gospel with Suman in a way he can relate to and comprehend is a challenge. God, however, delivered a way through Suman's desire for dual citizenship. In our next conversation, I will share with Suman how he and his family can become citizens of heaven. I pray that soon we can celebrate his new eternal citizenship! Gospel conversations lead to gospel invitations, which lead to gospel celebrations. What qualifies as a gospel celebration?

CELEBRATE GOSPEL PARTNERSHIPS

In 2010, Barna released personal evangelism research that revealed: "Among the interesting facets of the research was that just 1% of believers claim to have the gift of evangelism (down from 4% five years ago)."[xx] If only 1% of believers claim to have the gift of evangelism, then does that dismiss the other 99% of believers? The danger revealed by this statistic is the temptation of the 99% to justify not entering gospel conversations. Justifying the lack of gospel conversations may be popular, but it is not biblical. In 2 Timothy 4:5, Paul wrote, "As for you, always be sober-minded, endure suffering, do the work of an evangelist, fulfill your ministry." We cannot celebrate gospel partnerships if we eliminate gospel partnerships by 99%. 100% of believers are called to enter gospel conversations.

Paul encouraged Philemon to celebrate their gospel partnership by receiving Onesimus. In Philemon 17, Paul penned, "So if you consider me your *partner*, receive him as you would receive me" (emphasis mine). Paul's request was based upon a reciprocal partnership in the gospel. Regarding the depth of this partnership, Gerald Peterman surmised, "**Partner** is the equivalent of co-worker (v.1)—one who both receives and also spreads the gospel." [xxi]

Is Paul asking too much of Philemon? To ask Philemon to refrain from executing Onesimus is one thing. To ask Philemon to forgive Onesimus is another. But to ask Philemon to reconcile with Onesimus is something different altogether! The forgiven must forgive, but must the forgiven reconcile? The Bible reminds all believers that God "gave us the ministry of reconciliation" (2 Corinthians 5:18).

Gospel reconciliation between Philemon and Onesimus required both men to participate. Some commentators hold that Onesimus' hand delivered Paul's letter. Mark Dever wrote:

So that is Onesimus—the slave who stole, fled, and found

Paul; and in finding Paul, he found Christ and found his way back home. Now, Onesimus would turn up at Philemon's house with nothing but a letter from Paul in his hand. Can you imagine the former slave standing in the doorway as his former employer opens the door—needing forgiveness, helpless to repay, cared for only by someone far away in prison. In one sense, the destitution of this former slave is incomparable. He can offer nothing, and he deserves punishment. Yet there he stands, with no excuses to make.[xxii]

Paul did not merely ask Philemon to receive Onesimus. He asked Philemon to receive his runaway slave as he would receive Paul. How would Philemon receive Paul? Would he execute, beat, or treat Paul as a slave? Of course not. Philemon would roll out the red carpet and welcome Paul with arms wide open. He would put him in the finest room with Wi-Fi, Netflix, Hulu, and Amazon Prime.

Yes, Paul asked much of Philemon. In fact, there was little else left to ask. If Philemon did what Paul asked and received Onesimus as he would Paul, then Onesimus' slavery ends. If, in Christ, we do what Paul asks, there is nothing left to enslave. We would all be set free by gospel reconciliation.

Speaking on a more personal level, it is my experience, as a pastor, that pastors may be the most insecure creatures on earth. I am a pastor who consistently wrestles with insecurity. A grateful attitude and celebratory spirit is helpful in the battle against insecurity. Paul was not taunting Timothy when he wrote, "I have fought the good fight. I have finished the race, I have kept the faith." (2 Timothy 4:7). Paul was not saying, "In your face, Timothy, I beat you to the finish!" We are not called to compete in the Christian race; we are called to complete the race. Pastors and churches, we are not in a competition! Let's celebrate gospel partnerships! Gospel celebrations begin when we celebrate gospel partnerships.

CELEBRATE GOSPEL RELATIONSHIPS

Jesus implored his disciples to celebrate gospel relationships. In Luke 15:7, Jesus said, "Just so, I tell you, there will be more joy in heaven over one sinner who repents than over ninety-nine righteous persons who need no repentance." Again, Jesus told his disciples, "Just so, I tell you, there is joy before the angels of God over one sinner who repents" (Luke 15:10). Jesus expects his followers to celebrate what is eternal, which includes gospel relationships. Celebrating gospel relationships begins in a relationship with Jesus.

The apostle Paul offered one of the clearest pictures of redemption when he wrote, "If he has wronged you at all, or owes you anything, charge that to my account. I, Paul, write this with my own hand: I will repay it" (Philemon 18-19). Referencing Paul's statement to Philemon on behalf of Onesimus, Knute Larson commented:

> Pictures of Christ's redemption present themselves in the ordinary occurrences of life. Here Paul acted the Christ-figure, identifying with the accused so strongly that his debt became his own. But, like all of us before God, Onesimus cannot pay his debt. So Paul accepted it as his own—just as Christ did for all humankind upon the cross.[xxiii]

What a picture of redemption! Onesimus, no longer a slave but a brother in Christ, may have been *willing* to repay his debt, but he was not *able*. At the same time, Paul recognized that a debt was owed, but there was no way that Onesimus, a runaway slave, would be *able* to repay his debt. Paul did not ask Philemon to pretend that he suffered no loss. He did not ask Philemon to ignore, deny, or forget about Onesimus stealing from him, running away from him, and hurting him. Whether or not Onesimus stole from Philemon, the slave owner had to cover the work responsibilities of Onesimus. Paul acknowledged that Philemon may be without because Onesimus ran away. The apostle Paul considered what the one man owed and what the other man was owed.

When Jesus died on the cross, He satisfied the wrath of God and justified all sinners who believe in Him. Jesus considered both the wrath of God and the sin of man. On the night before His death, Jesus did not pray on the Mount of Olives, "Father, the sins of people are not that bad. Let's just look the other way." Jesus prayed, "Father, if you are willing, remove this cup from me. Nevertheless, not my will, but yours be done" (Luke 22:42). Jesus understood there was no way that we could repay our sin debt and satisfy the wrath of God.

My mother is cooler than the other side of the pillow. After my father's death in 1984, my twenty-nine-year-old mother raised three children on her own. If my mother calculated all the money it cost to raise three children and called in what we owed her, there is no way we could pay.

God is Holy. He cannot co-exist with sin. God the Father called in the sin debt of all mankind on a cross called Calvary. God the Son paid it all. Paul pointed out to Philemon that "I, Paul, write this with my own hand: I will repay it" (Philemon 19). Paul did not call on Timothy, Titus, Epaphras, or some other brother in Christ to commit to pay Onesimus' sin debt. By his own hand, Paul committed to pay. Jesus did not call on an angel to pay our sin debt. Jesus did not call on us to pay our sin debt. Jesus did not call on Moses or Elijah to pay our sin debt. By His own nail-scarred hands, Jesus paid it all. Elvina M. Hall wrote these words: "Jesus paid it all, All to Him I owe; Sin had left a crimson stain, He washed it white as snow."[xxiv] Should we not celebrate our gospel relationship with God the Father through God the Son?

In Philemon 19, Paul told Philemon "to say nothing of your owing me even your own self." Paul upheld that Philemon was owed a lot, but he also reminded Philemon of what he owed Paul. The apostle led Philemon to Christ. In essence, Paul is saying, "Whatever Onesimus owes you will never compare to what you owe me."

True enough, you may be owed a lot by someone in your life who hurt you. What you are owed, however huge the debt may be, will never compare to what you owe the Lord Jesus Christ. Celebrate the One who paid your debt. Celebrate your gospel relationship with God the Father through God the Son.

CELEBRATE GOSPEL FELLOWSHIP

Gospel celebrations are realized as we celebrate gospel partnerships, gospel relationships, and gospel fellowship. Is what you celebrate on earth being celebrated in heaven? Do you celebrate the eternal or the temporal? Do you celebrate things above or things below? Do you celebrate the spiritual or the physical? Living in SEC college football country reveals that too many followers of Jesus celebrate football champion-ships more than gospel fellowship. What an indict-ment on the local church! Jesus urged His disciples, "Do not rejoice in this, that the spirits are subject to you, but rejoice that your names are written in heav-en" (Luke 10:20).

Paul desired to celebrate the gospel fellowship between Onesimus and Philemon. In Philemon 20, Paul declared, "Yes, brother, I want some benefit from you in the Lord. Refresh my heart in Christ." John MacArthur added, "By forgiving Onesimus, Philemon would benefit Paul in the Lord by bringing him joy be-cause of his example of obedience and love to the church."[xxv]

At first glance, it may seem that Paul was butter-ing up Philemon in an effort to get his request for Onesimus granted. Was Paul's address of Philemon as "beloved fellow worker" (Philemon 1), "my brother" (Philemon 7), "partner" (Philemon 17), and "brother" (Philemon 20) a manipulation ploy? David E. Garland argues, "Paul is not trying to soften up Philemon with praise before broaching the topic of Onesimus' status."[xxvi]

Was Paul praising Philemon too much? Paul knew that Philemon was not merely a good man, but he was also a godly man. Paul praised Philemon not for being a good man in the flesh, but for being a godly man in Christ. By praising Philemon's faith in Christ and love for the saints, Paul was not praising Philemon. He was praising Christ in Philemon. Quoting the prophet Jeremiah, Paul wrote, "Let the one who boasts, boast in the Lord" (1 Corinthians 1:31). Let him keep on boasting in the Lord! Let him never stop boasting in the Lord!

Why should we never stop boasting in the Lord? Jesus' birth on this earth allowed us to be born from above. Jesus' life brought life to this life. Jesus' cross shamed our shame. Jesus' death put death to death. Jesus' resurrection resurrected resurrection. Why would you ever stop boasting in the Lord?

We will not praise Christ too much because we cannot praise Christ enough! Our praise of Christ will never be on our lips too much because our praise of Christ will never be on our lips enough!

Thom Rainer reminds pastors and church leaders, "The more you celebrate evangelism in the church, the more it will happen in the church."[xxvii] Capture the story of how a person came to Christ, and tell it during their baptism. Share all the different ministries and people God used to connect that person to Christ. Encourage the new believer to share their story with family and friends. Make a big deal out of telling your church how people are being connected to Christ. Never stop celebrating gospel partnerships, gospel relationships, and gospel fellowship. The celebration of what God has done through evangelism leads to God's glorification as highlighted in Philemon 21-25.

5

Gospel Congregations...

LEAD TO GOD'S GLORIFICATION

Confident of your obedience, I write to you, knowing that you will **do even more than I say**. *At the same time,* **prepare a guest room for me, for I am hoping that through your prayers I will be graciously given to you**. **Epaphras,** *my fellow prisoner in Christ Jesus, sends greetings to you, and so do* **Mark, Aristarchus, Demas, and Luke,** *my fellow workers. The* **grace of the Lord Jesus Christ be with your spirit.**

Philemon 21-25

JESUS ASKS MUCH BUT GIVES MORE

Lee Strobel uses the following illustration to demonstrate the human rebellious nature that makes clear biblical truths ambiguous.

> Imagine a daughter and her boyfriend going out for a Coke on a school night. The father says to her, 'You must be home before eleven.' It gets to be 10:45 p.m. and the two of them are still having a great time. They don't want the evening to end, so suddenly they begin to have difficulty interpreting the father's instructions: What did he really mean when he said, 'You must be home **before** eleven?' Did he literally mean us, or was he talking about you in a general sense, like people in general? Was he saying, in effect, 'As a general rule, people must be home before eleven?' Or was he just making the observation that 'Generally, people are in their homes before eleven?' I mean, he wasn't very clear, was he? And what did he mean by, 'You must be **home** before

eleven?' He didn't specify whose home. It could be anybody's home. Maybe he meant it figuratively. Remember the old saying, 'Home is where the heart is'? My heart is right here, so doesn't that mean I'm already home? And what did he really mean when he said, 'You must be home before **eleven**?' Did he mean that in an exact, literal sense? Besides, he never specified 11:00 p.m. or 11:00 a.m. And he wasn't really clear on whether he was talking about Central Standard Time or Eastern Time...When you think about it, it's always before the next eleven. So with all these ambiguities, we can't really be sure what he meant at all. If he can't make himself more clear, we certainly can't be held responsible.[xxviii]

Did Jesus really mean what He said? Did Jesus really say what He meant? When Jesus said, "If anyone would come after me, let him deny himself and take up his cross daily, and follow me" (Luke 9:23), did He really mean it? Did Jesus raise the bar or lower the bar? In his book *Rediscovering Discipleship*, Robby Gallaty wrote, "Jesus refused to lower the requirements for following him. Quite the contrary, when the multitudes praised him, he raised expectations and drove them away."xxix Jesus really did say what He meant, and really did mean what He said.

Jesus asks *much of His* followers, but He gives *more to His* followers. Jesus asked much of Paul. In Acts 9:16, Jesus said of Paul, "For I will show him how much he must suffer for the sake of my name." As Paul suffered for the sake of the gospel, he pleaded with Jesus to remove a thorn in his flesh, in effect, that it "should leave" him (2 Corinthians 12:8). Jesus responded, "My grace is sufficient for you, for my power is made perfect in weakness" (2 Corinthians 12:9). Jesus' grace saves us, sanctifies us, and sustains us. Jesus gives more grace!

Paul asked much of Philemon. In fact, Paul expected Philemon to do more than he asked. In Philemon 21, Paul declared, "Confident of your obedience, I write to you, knowing that you will do even more than I say."

So far, Paul asked Philemon to refrain from executing Onesimus, to forgive him, and be joyfully reconciled to him. What more could Paul expect from Philemon?

Paul may have been unable to ask more of Philemon, but the gospel of Jesus asks much more. The gospel could have asked Philemon to set Onesimus free from being a slave. The gospel could have asked Philemon to adopt Onesimus as a son. John Phillips commented, "How could he (Philemon) possibly do *more*? Well, he could adopt Onesimus as his own son! That would be the ultimate act of Christlikeness."[xxx] The gospel of Jesus asked much of Philemon and the gospel congregation that met in his house, but the gospel of Jesus gave more.

JESUS WILL RETURN FOR GOSPEL CONGREGATIONS
People assemble and congregate for a host of common interests, hobbies, passions, or purposes. Baseball tournaments, football games, musical concerts, and seasonal festivals are a few examples of events where like-minded people gather. In Philemon

1-2, Paul wrote, "To Philemon our beloved fellow worker and Apphia our sister and Archippus our fellow soldier, and *the church in your house*" (emphasis mine). Philemon hosted a gospel congregation in his house.

What is a gospel congregation? A gospel congregation consists of gathering a group of people who are eternally connected by grace alone, through faith alone, in Christ alone. Followers of Jesus Christ do not congregate *to be* a Garmin congregation, a Gatorade congregation, a GAP Kids congregation, a GE congregation, a G.I. Joe congregation, a GOP congregation, or a Google congregation. Followers of Jesus congregate because *they are* gospel congregations.

Why is it important to be part of a gospel congregation? Jesus will return for gospel congregations. Jesus will not return for any and every assembly, bunch, crowd, flock, gathering, huddle, or multitude. Jesus will return only for gospel assemblies, gospel bunches, gospel crowds, gospel flocks, gospel gatherings, gospel huddles, and gospel multitudes. Jesus will return for gospel congregations.

Paul told Philemon that he would return to his house sooner than later. In Philemon 22, Paul said, "At the same time, prepare a guest room for me, for I am hoping that through your prayers I will be graciously given to you." Paul would not return to any ol' house in Colossae. He would return to Philemon's house, the very house where a gospel congregation gathered.

How can we make a parallel between Paul returning to Philemon's house with Jesus returning for his church? By taking on Onesimus' debt, Paul already pointed us to the redemptive work of Christ. Furthermore, the second-person pronoun "you" in Philemon 22 is not singular, but plural. In Philemon 21, the "you" is singular, as Paul is addressing Philemon specifically; however, in Philemon 22, the "you" is plural, as Paul is addressing the entire gospel congregation that meets in Philemon's house. Paul, then, asked this gospel congregation "to prepare" for his sooner- rather-than-later arrival. Jesus said, "Behold, I am coming soon" (Revelation 22:12). Jesus will return sooner than later for gospel congregations.

The Babylon Bee satirically reported:

> In a stunning leak Monday, sources in heaven claimed to have 'reliable information' that the triumphant return of Jesus Christ will occur during the deciding Game 7 of the World Series between the Cleveland Indians and the Chicago Cubs...sources added that the Second Coming will take place during the final inning, as one of the teams comes agonizingly close to winning the World Series. Cleveland fans have waited since 1948 to see a baseball championship, and Cubs fans have not witnessed a World Series title since 1908. It appears both fan bases will have to continue waiting.[xxxi]

Obviously, Jesus did not return during the 2016 World Series. No one knows *when* Jesus will return, but all should know He *is* returning.

Are you ready for Jesus' soon return? What do you need to remove from your internet history, DVR, playlist, and social media posts in order to honor Him? Are you a part of a gospel congregation? If you are not a part of a gospel congregation, then you are not ready. We can disobey the gospel, but we cannot delay the gospel. Jesus will return for gospel congregations.

JESUS IS REIGNING OVER GOSPEL CONGREGATIONS

What does a gospel congregation look like? Gospel congregations consist of people who confess Jesus as Lord. As Lord, Jesus is reigning over the people who constitute gospel congregations. In Philemon, Paul mentioned the names Timothy, Philemon, Apphia, Archippus, Epaphras, Mark, Aristarchus, Demas, and Luke. The names of these saints represent gospel relationships in Paul's life. One of Paul's favorite phrases "in Christ" (Philemon 23) communicates Jesus was reigning over these saints. Just as Jesus reigned over gospel congregations in Paul's day, Jesus reigns over gospel congregations today.

Different personalities, different stages of life, different generations, different economic classes, and different ethnicities all personify the people in gospel congregations. In Philemon 23-24, Epaphras, Mark, Aristarchus, Demas, and Luke were different people who followed the same person, Jesus.

What do we know about each of these men? John Phillips offered the following synopsis:

> Marcus was a Jerusalem Jew, Aristarchus was a Thessalonian, and Luke was possibly a Macedonian or a Syrian. Mark and Luke both wrote gospels—Mark the Gospel of Jesus as God's Servant; Luke the Gospel of Jesus as Man's Savior. Aristarchus, like Epaphras, was Paul's 'fellow captive.' Demas—well, Demas was soon to defect because he loved the present evil world.[xxxii]

Epaphras is described as "my fellow prisoner in Christ" (Philemon 23). Regarding Epaphras, Paul wrote, "Epaphras, who is one of you, a servant of Christ Jesus, greets you, always struggling on your behalf in his prayers, that you may stand mature and fully assured in all the will of God" (Colossians 4:12).

Mark and Paul had a falling out. J. Vernon McGee commented, "Remember that Paul wouldn't take John Mark with him on his second missionary journey. But Paul had been wrong about Mark, and now he was able to say that Mark was profitable to him in his ministry."[xxxiii]

Aristarchus was one of Paul's "fellow workers" (Philemon 24). Although little else is known about him, Paul's distinction of Aristarchus speaks of his devotion to the gospel.

Rounding the list of names are Demas and Luke. Finding these two names next to one another is ironic. Paul said of Demas, "Demas, in love with this present world, has deserted me and gone to Thessalonica" (2 Timothy 4:10). In the very next verse, Paul said of Luke, "Luke alone is with me" (2 Timothy 4:11). Demas deserted Paul; yet, after everyone else deserted Paul, Luke was the only one who remained with him.

The reality that Jesus was reigning over these men connected them to one another. Each of these men represent different personalities, life stages, economic statuses, and backgrounds. At the same time, each of these men played an important role in the gospel congregation.

What does it look like to be a gospel congregation? Jesus is reigning over gospel congregations. Concerning the importance of each member of a local congregation, Thom Rainer wrote, "With church membership, everyone has a role or function. That is why some are hands, feet, ears, or eyes. We are all different, but we are necessary parts of the whole."[xxxiv] What function or role are you accomplishing under the Lordship of Jesus in a gospel congregation?

JESUS RESTORES GOSPEL CONGREGATIONS

How does a congregation become and remain a gospel congregation? The only way any congregation will ever become and remain a gospel congregation is by the unmerited, undeserved grace of God alone. In Philemon 25, Paul concluded, "The *grace* of the Lord Jesus Christ be with your spirit." Thankfully, Paul did not say, "The *justice* of the Lord Jesus Christ be with your spirit." How hopeless we would be if God's *justice* not His *grace* was with our spirit!

Praise Jesus that His purpose is to offer His grace to helpless, hopeless sinners who form gospel congregations. Justice means we *get what we deserve.* Mercy means we *don't get what we deserve.* Grace means we *get what we don't deserve.* God restores gospel congregations by His grace. God's grace is greater than our worst. No sin is beyond the reach of God's grace. God's grace is greater than our best. No person is without the need for God's grace.

Praise Jesus that His power is available to gospel congregations. Paul's use of "Lord" (Philemon 25) highlights the power and authority of Jesus. Jesus said, "All authority in heaven and on earth has been given to me" (Matthew 28:18). All means *all,* y'all! Jesus has authority over every gospel transformation, gospel conversation, gospel invitation, gospel celebration, and gospel congregation. He has authority over every person that enters a gospel conversation. Jesus has authority over you to share the gospel and authority over the person to whom you will share. He has authority over every person in a gospel congregation.

Praise Jesus that His person is available to gospel congregations. Pertaining to Jesus' person, Paul uses the name "Jesus" (Philemon 25). In Matthew 1:21, Joseph was told, "She (Mary) will bear a son, and you shall call his name Jesus, for he will save his people from their sins." The humanity of Jesus allowed Him not only to identify with us but to save us. Jesus is our Savior, and He alone sustains us.

Praise Jesus that His position is His alone. Paul described Jesus' position by using the title "Christ" (Philemon 25). Jesus alone is Messiah. He alone is God in the flesh. The deity of Jesus allowed Him to live a perfect life that we could never live.

In Philemon 25, Jesus' purpose, power, person, and position reminds us that He alone is willing and able to restore gospel congregations. Jesus will return for gospel congregations. Jesus is reigning over gospel congregations. Jesus restores gospel congregations.

GATHER TO JESUS TO SCATTER FOR JESUS

The Magic Kingdom was so magical that my four-year-old, Belle, inadvertently left her stuffed companion,

B, in the park. After an exhausting day in the park, as we were walking through the hotel lobby on the way to our room, Belle began to wail. "B! Where's B?" B was lost. Immediately, I became intimately acquainted with Disney World's Lost and Found department. Every hour, I called them to see if B had been dropped off. About midnight, they told me that a stuffed bear may have been found.

Early the next morning, I caught a bus from the hotel to lost and found. The pleasant lady driving the bus boasted that Disney World had over a 90% recovery rate of lost items. A glimmer of hope was in the cool January air. Upon arriving at lost and found, I noticed I was one of about three dads. The lost and found office had the feel of a shameful place where irresponsible parents were held accountable. One of the dads looked at me and said, "What are you in for?"

Sitting behind the lost and found desk was a uniformed security guard. "Next!" One of the dads in front of me shimmied up to the desk. The security guard interrogated him with a parade of questions. Then, it was my turn to face the intimidating guard.

After a grueling cross-examination, the guard disappeared into the next room and re-appeared with B in tow. We were on the positive side of the 90% recovery rate. I had never been so excited to see a stuffed bear and couldn't wait for Belle and B to be reunited.

Jesus said, "I am the way, and the truth, and the life. No man comes to the Father except through me" (John 14:6). The exclusivity of Christ is foundational truth. No one, 0%, will be gathered to the Father unless they come through the Son. It is also true that everyone, 100%, will be gathered to the Father who come through the Son. Disney World may have a 90% recovery rate of lost items, but 100% of the lost who come to Jesus will be found.

We gather as local churches because we are gospel congregations. We scatter as the church to have gospel conversations. People must be pointed to Jesus. People must be told, "Behold, the Lamb of God who takes away the sin of the world" (John 1:29). All of this starts with a conversation. So, go, engage someone in conversation!

The biblical basis for moving any and every conversation to a gospel conversation is verified in Paul's letter to Philemon. Gospel transformation leads to gospel conversations. Gospel conversations lead to gospel invitations. Gospel invitations lead to gospel celebrations. Gospel celebrations lead to gospel congregations. Gospel congregations lead to God's glorification. God's glorification is the goal of gospel congregations. Gospel congregations begin by way of gospel conversations. Engaging the lost in everyday life begins with a conversation.

6

God's Glorification...

IS THE GOAL

As for you, always be sober-minded, endure suffering, **do the work of an evangelist, fulfill your ministry. For I am already being poured out as a drink offering, and the time of my departure has come. I have fought the good fight, I have finished the race, I have kept the faith.** *Henceforth there is laid up for me the crown of righteousness, which the Lord, the righteous judge, will award to me on that Day, and not only to me but also to all who have loved his appearing.*

2 Timothy 4:5-8

WHY ENGAGE THE LOST IN EVERYDAY LIFE?

God's glory is the primary reason to engage the lost in everyday life. Jesus is not one Christ among many Christs. Jesus alone is the Christ. He alone is worthy of all the worship of every tongue, tribe, nation, and people. Evangelism in everyday life must be a priority because Jesus is worthy of every person's worship.

Was it a matter of months, weeks, days, or hours? How long did the Apostle Paul live after penning 2 Timothy? In 2 Timothy 4:6, Paul writes, "I am *already being poured out* as a drink offering and the *time of my departure has come.*" Tony Merida commented, "Based on the end of 2 Timothy, it seems Paul had already received a court hearing (2 Tim 4:16-18) and expected to be executed soon" (4:6-8).[xxxv] Paul concluded in 2 Timothy 18, "The Lord will rescue me from every evil deed and bring me safely home into his heavenly kingdom. *To him be glory forever and ever. Amen.*" At the end of his earthly life, Paul unveiled the goal of an evangelistic life: God's glorification.

Why is God's glorification the reason to engage the lost in everyday life? Since God is worthy of every person's worship in everyday life, then no person is ever worthless. All world religions, false gospels, traditions, and worldviews will leave people feeling worthless. Following Jesus alone gives purpose to everyday life!

Lifeway Research, in partnership with the Billy Graham Center for Evangelism, interviewed two thousand unchurched Americans, that is, people who have not attended a worship service in six months. According to the research, the unchurched are very open to a gospel conversation. Rainer concluded, "Almost eight out of ten unchurched Americans would welcome a gospel conversation. Another 12% would discuss it with some discomfort...We can't use the poor excuse that the unchurched really aren't interested in gospel conversations."[xxxvi] Jesus took the initiative to engage people. Jesus expects His Church to take the initiative and engage people for Him.

Paul, in his final words, implored Timothy to "do the work of an evangelist" (2 Timothy 4:5). The term "evangelism" can be understood as the work done by an evangelist. Paul describes evangelism as "work."

Is evangelism work? Alvin Reid describes the tension involved in the work of evangelism:

> You don't know how a person may respond when you share Christ. That thought alone brings some tension, right? Sometimes when you share Christ people raise objections—the thought of not being able to answer them brings tension as well (note: the Bible does not tell us we have to answer every question as many are frivolous, but we are to give reason for the hope within us)…Embrace tension, and sharing Christ becomes less a chore and more a joy.[xxxvii]

Yes, evangelism is work. Does evangelism work? Yes, evangelism works. Evangelism is work for the people of God, but it works for the glory of God.

Mid-week church services at Red Bank Baptist Church consist of orchestra rehearsal, choir rehearsal, student worship, children's worship, and a typical prayer meeting with Bible study. After enjoying a savory meal as a church family, families divide up in to their respective places of service on Wednesday night. The Wednesday before Christmas, the mid-week church gathering seemed to be no different. Until I met Wayne.

Wayne is a millennial who happens to be an attorney. Meeting Wayne for the first time, he said, "I felt compelled to come to this church tonight." His first time at Red Bank Baptist Church was also his first time back in any church in five years. Before arriving, Wayne pulled into the parking lot of other churches, but they had canceled mid-week services, as it was the week before Christmas.

When describing how he pulled into the parking lot of Red Bank Baptist, he said, "God led my car into the parking lot of this church." Wayne told me later that he had pulled into the parking lot and parked. He sat there a few minutes. He cranked the car and drove out of the parking lot to go back home. Halfway home, he turned the car around and drove back to the parking lot. A few people waved, and he got out of the car. One lady directed him to the Bible study where Wayne and I spoke for the first time.

The message that night was from Luke's gospel on the subject of Jesus (Jesus is a good subject to study). We looked at the truth that Jesus is the Lord of Life, the God of grace, and the Savior of sinners. Wayne told me later, "I just sat there and wept." Later that night he sent an email, which read, "It was nice to meet you tonight. Your message really hit home and I would like to speak to you further, if you have time. I felt compelled tonight to come to your church and I'm glad I did."

Two days later, Wayne and I had a gospel conversation over lunch. He revealed how tired he was of feeling empty, depressed, and fearful. Wayne spoke of what happened when he arrived home after the Bible study. He dropped to his knees, confessed his sins, and asked Jesus into his life. He said, "When I got up off my knees, a huge burden was lifted. I feel a sense of purpose. I feel alive. Jesus changed me, and I want Him to change me even more."

God saved Wayne. God led him to hear the gospel. He listened to the gospel. He asked questions about the gospel. He believed the gospel. Wayne discovered that he is not worthless and that Jesus is worthy! Jesus and Wayne are why we engage the lost in everyday life. Who is your Wayne?

HOW TO ENGAGE THE LOST IN EVERYDAY LIFE

Chattanooga is a hidden gem buried in East Tennessee. While pastoring in Chattanooga the past five years, I have realized that God has called my family to the Bible belt. The year 2016 marks the second time in three years that Chattanooga has been named the most Bible-minded city in the United States.[xxxviii] Bible-minded is not always synonymous, however, with Bible-believing or Bible-obeying. Christ followers in Chattanooga desperately need to engage Chattanoogans in gospel conversations. God's gospel is for every tribe, tongue, language, and people; including the people in your city. People in all cities and communities need to hear the gospel. How do you engage the lost in everyday life in your city and community?

Another thing I have learned while living in Chattanooga the past five years is that God has called my family to Volunteer country. East Tennessee loves the University of Tennessee, or as often referred to, "UT". Although I am not a UT fan, living in UT country means no more trouble spelling DeUTeronomy.

The University of Tennessee's legendary quarter-back, Peyton Manning, retired from professional football in March of 2016. During his retirement speech, Peyton said, "When I was drafted by the Colts, Indianapolis was a basketball and a car racing town but it didn't take long for the Colts to convert the city and state of Indiana into football evangelists."[xxxix]

What can Peyton Manning's "football evangelism" teach us about engaging the lost in everyday life? Out of respect for Number Eighteen's eighteen-year ca-reer and in light of the Bible's command to "do the work of an evangelist," I offer eighteen helps as you engage the lost in everyday life.[xl]

1. **Get started.** Peyton said the decision to play his senior year in Knoxville was "one of the smartest decisions I've ever made." Eventually, Peyton did start playing professional football. Getting in the game of sharing your faith by engaging the lost in everyday life won't happen until you get started. Get started by having a conversation. Look and listen for a way to connect with a person in a conversation. Through that conversation, ask God to provide a way to guide the conversation to the gospel.

2. **Failures are not final.** Peyton Manning holds many professional quarterback records, including the rookie record for the most interceptions. Peyton's failed reception attempts didn't stop him from delivering the ball. Maybe you have tried to engage a person with the gospel but failed to communicate the gospel clearly. Maybe you have tried to engage a person with the gospel but you were interrupted. Don't give up! Keep delivering the gospel!

3. **Remain coachable.** Speaking of his National Football League coaches, Peyton said, "Over my NFL career, I've had five coaches who have helped me become better at my craft and have helped me become a better human being: Jim Mora, Tony Dungy, Jim Caldwell, John Fox, and Gary Kubiak." His gratitude for his coaches highlights the fact that Peyton remained coachable. Remaining coachable is critically important as you continue to engage the lost in everyday life. Keep growing more in your faith, so you will keep sharing your faith more.

4. **God's Word is our playbook.** Can you imagine the number of playbooks Peyton has memorized throughout his career? Of all those playbooks, Peyton referenced 2 Timothy 4:7 in his retirement speech, "I have fought the good fight, I have finished the race, I have kept the faith." God's Word is our evangelism playbook. Meditate on it. Memorize it. Obey it. Live it. Share it.

5. **The game, not the goal, changes.** Eighteen years is an extra long career in the National Football League, considering the average career length is about 3.3 years.[xli] Many changes may occur over the course of eighteen years in the game of football, like rule changes and players' safety. Yet, the goal of football never changes. As former NFL coach Herman Edwards ranted, "You play to win the game!"[xlii] The way we engage people with the gospel may change, but the message and the goal of the gospel never changes. The goal of engaging the lost in everyday life is to win souls for the glory of God.

6. **The mission is greater than the mission's greatest.** The sport of football is even greater than one of football's greatest players, Peyton Manning. The Great Commission is the greatest mission for followers of Christ. Making much of the God who made us and the Christ who remade us is our greatest mission as we make disciples. Even the greatest disciplemaker on

earth is not greater than the greatest mission under heaven to make disciples.

7. **You are not alone.** During his retirement speech, Peyton named family, players, coaches, friends, and fans who joined him on his football journey. At times, following Christ will be lonely, but being lonely is not the same thing as being alone. When you are lonely, remember you are never alone as you share the gospel. Identify someone who can hold you accountable as you share your faith. Ask someone else to invest in your life by praying with you as you engage the lost with the gospel. Invest in another person who needs to be engaging the lost for Christ.

8. **Setbacks don't have to set you back.** When speaking about the ups and downs in football, Peyton said, "Football has taught me not to be led by obstructions and setbacks...." Sin is a setback, but sin doesn't have to set you back in sharing Jesus with the lost. Before you sin, resist giving into that temptation by resting in

God's grace. When you sin, repent and rest in God's grace. Don't allow sin to set you back from engaging the lost; rather, allow God's grace to set you up to engage the lost.

9. **Include your family.** When I became a New Orleans Saints fan in 1981, Archie Manning, Peyton Manning's dad, quarterbacked the Saints. Peyton's older brother, Cooper Manning, played football. Peyton Manning played football. Eli Manning, Peyton's younger brother, still plays football. The Manning family is a football family. Is your family a gospel family? Do you involve your family in sharing the gospel of Jesus? As a family, do you talk about the gospel? As a family, do you pray for lost people? As a family, do you host other families in your home for dinner? As a family, do you share the gospel with others? Share your faith as a family!

10. **Endure to the end.** Endurance is a theme in 2 Timothy as Paul is imploring Timothy to endure to the end by doing the work of an evangelist.

Peyton, addressing the timing of his retirement, said, "After eighteen years, it's time." He endured to the end of his football career. You are never too old to share your faith. You are never too "out of touch" to share your faith. Endure to the end by sharing your faith to the end.

11. **Peyton played using his unique personality.** God made no two quarterbacks with the same personality. Peyton played using his own personality and no one else's. No two followers of Jesus have the same personality. The gospel never changes, but the personalities who share the gospel are never the same. Be the best you can be by being all God made you to be in Christ. Share the gospel through your own personality.

12. **Share one conversation at a time.** Peyton led the Colts to win at least 12 games in seven consecutive seasons. Still, Peyton could only play one game at a time. Jesus, as the Incarnate Word, engaged people one conversation at a time. Don't be overwhelmed at the

vast lostness around you. Combat that lostness by having one gospel conversation at a time. Engage the lost in everyday life - one conversation at a time. Ask God to give you opportunity, boldness, and compassion to have at least one gospel conversation each day.

13. **God is aware and cares.** Peyton closed his retirement speech with this blessing, "God bless all of you and God bless football." Does God care about football? God absolutely cares about the people involved in football, because God is aware of the people involved in football. God absolutely cares about you engaging the lost in everyday life, because God is aware of the people involved. Be encouraged that God is for you engaging the lost for Him!

14. **Finishing doesn't mean you are finished.** Peyton left the football field, but he has something left to offer off the football field. He said, "There's a scripture reading, 2 Timothy 4:7: 'I have fought the good fight and I have finished the race. I have kept the faith.' Well, I've fought

a good fight. I've finished my football race...."
Although his football race is over, Peyton's life's
race is not over. As a follower of Christ, you
never retire from following Christ. If you are still
breathing, God is not finished with you!

15. **Leave a living legacy.** Of Peyton Manning,
Tom Brady said, "Congratulations Peyton, on
an incredible career. You changed the game
forever and made everyone around you better.
It's been an honor."[xliii] Peyton has left a living
legacy in the world of football. In all of creation
under heaven, only the souls of men and the
Word of God remain forever. Our mission is to
share the Word of God with the souls of men.
Leave a living legacy by sharing the gospel of
Jesus for it lasts forever!

16. **Be grateful.** Surmising his thoughts about the
game of football, coaches, organizations, players, and fans, Peyton declared, "Grateful is the
word that comes to my mind." His gratitude for
the game shows that Peyton never got over the
game. One of the ways to guard against never

getting over the gospel is to express gratitude for the gospel. Are you expressing gratitude for the gospel? Be grateful as you share the gospel. Show that you are grateful when you share the gospel by smiling.

17. **Jesus is the Hero of the gospel.** Addressing his preparation and work ethic, Peyton shared:

Pundits will speculate that my effort and drive over the past 18 years were about mastery and working to master every aspect of the NFL game. Well, don't believe them. Because every moment, every drop of sweat, every bleary-eyed night of preparation, every note I took and every frame of film I watched was about one thing, reverence for this game.

Peyton's reverence for the game drove the future Hall of Fame quarterback to be his best. What drives you to be your best? What is your motivation? Jesus is the hero of the gospel. Jesus is the reason we share. Jesus is the reason we engage the lost in everyday life.

18. Have fun. Peyton's official retirement announcement even had a flavor of fun in it as he said, "There is just something about 18 years. Eighteen is a good number and today I retire from pro football." As you continue to engage the lost in everyday life, don't take yourself so seriously. Peyton didn't. Enjoy sharing the joy of Christ with the lost. Have fun engaging the lost in everyday life!

So What Now?

As you've now read in this book about gospel conversations, my prayer is that you will take what you've learned and put it into practice. I hope you will intentionally decide to share the Good News of Jesus Christ as you engage in conversations every day. As a ministry, Replicate is focused on equipping the local church to make disciples who make disciplemakers. We would love to help you as you follow Jesus's command to make disciples. Visit www.replicate.org for more information and free resources.

The following information explains the key ways Replicate can equip you and your church:

The Growing Up Series

01. GROWING UP: HOW TO BE A DISCIPLE WHO MAKES DISCIPLES

I think I'm a lot like you. There was a time in my life when I wanted to grow in my faith but just didn't know how.

- I owned a Bible but didn't understand it.
- I heard others pray but didn't know how to communicate with God.
- I wanted to share my faith with others but didn't know where to start.
- I had friends at church but lacked deep relationships with anyone.
- I wanted to hide God's Word in my heart but lacked a plan for memorization.
- I read the Scriptures but didn't know how to apply them.

Maybe this is where you are today. One day my life changed forever. What was the turning point? *I realized the importance and power of discipleship.*

Two men took the time to invest in my life: David Platt—author of *Radical* and *Follow Me*, as well as the foreword of my book—and Tim LaFleur. Since then, I have read nearly every book on discipleship, searching for answers to my questions.

Now I want to share my findings with you. *Growing Up* takes the guesswork out of growing closer to the Lord and equipping others to do the same. This book has the potential to change your life!

02. FIRMLY PLANTED: A BLUEPRINT FOR CULTIVATING A FORTIFIED FAITH

Why is spiritual growth so complicated?

Are you one of the many Christians desiring a closer relationship with God but having no idea where to begin? Then this book is for you! In biblical, practical, and simple terms, Robby Gallaty shares a road map for spiritual maturity. The book addresses topics such as these:

- How you can be sure of your salvation
- Why your identity in Christ affects everything you do

- How to overcome the three enemies that cripple a Christian's growth
- A battle plan for gaining victory over temptation
- The indispensable spiritual discipline every believer must foster

03. BEARING FRUIT: WHAT HAPPENS WHEN GOD'S PEOPLE GROW

Bearing Fruit is the third book in the *Growing Up* series. In this book, we will look at how God grows believers. We'll discuss how Christians can know they are saved, overcome temptation, as well as look at spiritual warfare from an internal and external perspective. *Bearing Fruit* is applicable for new and mature believers alike. Don't miss it. Be sure to follow replicate.org for all the latest information. Coming fall 2017.

CUSTOMIZED EQUIPPING

Every church wants to obey Jesus's command to make disciples.

Often, we find our ministry is geared to get as many people in the front door of our church as possible. The challenge is that people are leaving through the back door of the church just as quickly as they enter the front. We need to grow our people beyond simply being inviters to being investors. We teach them to share their faith, but they need to learn to share their lives.

Jesus devoted 90 percent of his time to discipling twelve men" (—Robby Gallaty).

Jesus used a radically different approach than what we see in the church today. We devote so much of our time to evangelistic strategies that we often neglect discipleship. Disciplemaking is both evangelism *and* discipleship. We need to show our people that Jesus didn't just save them *from* something (evangelism) but *for* something (discipleship). We must focus on both. We need a strategy founded on biblical principles that is practical and reproducible.

Imagine seeing a multiplying, disciplemaking movement ignite in your church or ministry.

Discipleship isn't a class you take, a program you attend, or a book you study; discipleship is the course of your life. Learn a tried-and-tested process for multiplying disciples in your ministry context. Our team can help you launch a disciplemaking movement in your church or ministry.

To connect with the Replicate Team about training in your context, go to replicate.org, or e-mail info@ replicate.org.

THE DISCIPLESHIP BLUEPRINT

The disciplemaking blueprint is a two-day experience that allows you to spend time in the context of a local church actively engaging in discipleship. You'll have the opportunity to spend time with staff as well as walk alongside members as you do the following:

1. Learn how to plan, formulate, and develop a disciplemaking culture in your church and its ministries (missions, women, and men)
2. Study Jesus's and other historical models for making disciples
3. Develop a comprehensive plan for raising up leaders in your church
4. Learn how to navigate issues that arise in your D-groups

5. Participate in a D-group led by an experienced disciplemaker
6. Consider principles and strategies for starting D-groups and multiplying mature believers in your context

www.replicate.org

End Notes

i.   Ray Ortlund, *The Gospel: How the Church Portrays the Beauty of Christ* (Wheaton, IL: Crossway, 2014), 15.

ii.   David Platt, *Radical: Taking Back Your Faith from the American Dream* (Colorado Springs, CO: Multnomah, 2010), 36.

iii.   Robby Gallaty, *MARCS of a Disciple: A Biblical Guide for Gauging Spiritual Growth* (Hendersonville, TN: Replicate Resources, 2016), 13.

iv.   John Phillips, *Exploring Colossians & Philemon* (Grand Rapids, MI: Kregel Publications, 2002), 250.

v.   Brooks, Philips, *Lectures on Preaching* (New York: E.P. Dutton, 1877).

vi.   Steve Gaines, *Share Jesus Like It Matters* (Tigerville, SC: Auxano Press, 2016), 70.

vii.   Robby Gallaty, *MARCS of a Disciple: A Biblical Guide for Gauging Spiritual Growth* (Hendersonville, TN: Replicate Resources, 2016), 13.

viii.	Kenneth Berding, *Biola Magazine*, http://magazine.biola.edu/article/14- spring/the-crisis-of-biblical-illiteracy/ Accessed 15 February 2017.

ix.	Dr. Chuck Herring's opening statement at the Garden of Gethsemane, January 2017.

x.	Gospel conversation with David and Dr. Chuck Herring in Jerusalem, January 2017.

xi.	Gospel conversation with David in Jerusalem, January 2017.

xii.	BobUnruh,WND,http://www.wnd.com/2016/07/russia-puts-lid-on-christians sharing-faith. Accessed 29 October 2016.

xiii.	Janet Sternberg, *New York Daily News*, http://www.nydailynews.com/life-style/texting-ruining-art-conversation-fear-losing-ability-traditional-face-to-face-conversations-article-1.1089679. Accessed 29 October 2016.

xiv.	Stephen Lutz, Breakout Session at Collegiate Collective Conference, 2013.

xv.	George Tanya Mbongko, Peace Rally in Cameroon Africa, 20 January 2016.

xvi. Bamileke – Religious and Expressive Culture, http://www.everyculture.com /Africa-Middle-East/Bamil-k-Religion-and-Expressive-Culture. html. Accessed 31 October 2016.

xvii. Thom Rainer, *The Unchurched Next Door* (Grand Rapids, MI: Zondervan, 2003), 25.

xviii. William C. Trenchard, *Complete Vocabulary Guide to the Greek New Testament* (Grand Rapids, MI: Zondervan, 1992), 53.

xix. Douglas J. Moo, *The Pillar New Testament Commentary: The Letters to the Colossians and to Philemon* (Grand Rapids, MI: William B. Eerdmans, 2008), 407.

xx. Ed Stetzer, *The Exchange,* http://www. christianitytoday.com/edstetzer/2010/july/ no-such-thing-as-gift-of-evangelism.html. Accessed 1 November 2016.

xxi. Gerald Peterman, *The Moody Bible Commentary: Philemon* (Chicago: Moody Publishers, 2014), 1917.

xxii. Mark Dever, *The Message of the New Testament* (Wheaton, IL: Crossway Books, 2005), 407.

xxiii.   Knute Larson, *Holman New Testament Commentary: I & II Thessalonians, I & II Timothy, Titus, Philemon* (Nashville, TN: Broadman & Holman, 2000), 408.

xxiv.   Elvina M. Hall, *Baptist Hymnal* (Nashville, TN: Lifeway Worship, 2008), 249.

xxv.   John MacArthur, *The MacArthur New Testament Commentary: Colossians & Philemon* (Chicago: Moody Publishers, 1992), 227.

xxvi.   David E. Garland, *The NIV Application Commentary: Colossians/Philemon* (Grand Rapids, MI: Zondervan, 1998), 318.

xxvii.   Thom Rainer, *Thom S. Rainer Growing Healthy Churches. Together*, http:// thomrainer. com/2017/01/renew-evangelistic-growth-church/. Accessed 11 January 2017.

xxviii. James Emery White, *Christ among Dragons* (Downers Grove, IL: InterVarsity Press, 2010), 177.

xxix.   Robby Gallaty, *Rediscovering Discipleship: Making Jesus' Final Words Our First Work* (Grand Rapids, MI: Zondervan, 2015), 171.

xxx. John Phillips, *Exploring Colossians & Philemon* (Grand Rapids, MI: Kregel Publications, 2002), 263.

xxxi. The Babylon Bee, http://babylonbee.com/news/second-coming-christ-scheduled-game-7-cubs-indians-world-series. Accessed 3 November 2016.

xxxii. John Phillips, *Exploring Colossians & Philemon* (Grand Rapids, MI: Kregel Publications, 2002), 264.

xxxiii. J. Vernon McGee, *Thru the Bible: 1 Corinthians through Revelation* (Nashville, TN: Thomas Nelson Publishers, 1983), 478.

xxxiv. Thom Rainer, *I Am A Church Member: Discovering the Attitude that Makes the Difference* (Nashville, TN: B&H Publishing Group, 2013), 12.

xxxv. Tony Merida, *Christ-Centered Exposition: Exalting Jesus in 2 Timothy* (Nashville, TN: B&H Publishing Group, 2013), 133.

xxxvi. Thom Rainer, *Thom S. Rainer Growing Healthy Churches. Together*, http://thomrainer.com/

2016/12/five-surprising-insights-unchurched/. Accessed 12 January 2017.

xxxvii. Alvin Reid, *The Tension of Evangelism*, http://www.thecgs.org/2017/01/the- tension-in-evangelism/. Accessed 12 January 2017.

xxxviii.American Bible Society, *The Most Bible-Minded Cities in America*, http:// www.americanbible.org/features/americas-most-bible-minded-cities. Accessed 17 January 2017.

xxxix. Peyton Manning, Transcript of Peyton Manning's Retirement Speech, http:// www.espn.com/blog/denver-broncos/post/_/id/19274/transcript-of-peyton-mannings-retirement-speech. Accessed 17 January 2017.

xl. All of Peyton's following quotes derive from his retirement speech. Peyton Manning, Transcript of Peyton Manning's Retirement Speech, http://www.espn.com/blog/denver-broncos/post/_/id/19274/transcript-of-peyton-mannings-retirement-speech. Accessed 17 January 2017.

xli. National Football League Players Association, *Average Playing Career Length in the NFL*, https://www.statista.com/statistics/240102/ average-player-career-length-in-the-national-football-league/. Accessed 17 January 2017.

xlii.   Doug Farrar, *10 Years Later*, Herm Edwards' 'You Play to Win the Game!!!' Rant still Resonates, http://sports.yahoo.com/blogs/shutdown-corner/10-years-later-herm-edwards-play-win-game-225650424--nfl.html. Accessed 17 January 2017.

xliii.   Tom Brady, *Tom Brady Congratulates Peyton Manning on Retirement*, https: //www.boston.com/sports/new-england-patriots/2016/03/06/tom-brady-congratulates-peyton-manning-on-retirement-you-changed-the-game-forever. Accessed 17 January 2017.

Made in the USA
Lexington, KY
19 January 2018